THE 5 LOVE LANGUAGES®

· OF CHILDREN ·

WORKBOOK

THE 5 LOVE LANGUAGES® OF CHILDREN

#1 *NEW YORK TIMES* BESTSELLER

Gary Chapman
Ross Campbell

WORKBOOK

NORTHFIELD PUBLISHING
CHICAGO

Developed with the assistance of Peachtree Publishing Services (www.peachtreeeditorial.com). Special thanks to Randy Southern.
Interior design: Erik M. Peterson
Cover design: Faceout Studio
Cover image of bokeh copyright © 2023 by Ole moda/Shutterstock (1469341238). All rights reserved.

ISBN: 978-0-8024-3294-0

We hope you enjoy this book from Northfield Publishing. Our goal is to provide high-quality, thought-provoking books and products that connect truth to your real needs and challenges. For more information on other books and products that will help you with all your important relationships, go to northfieldpublishing.com or write to:

Northfield Publishing
820 N. LaSalle Boulevard
Chicago, IL 60610

1 3 5 7 9 10 8 6 4 2

Printed in the United States of America

CONTENTS

INTRODUCTION

Welcome to a labor of love.

The twelve lessons in this book were created for one purpose: to strengthen and deepen your loving relationship with your children. The process won't be easy. Nothing worthwhile ever is. This study will pose some challenging questions. It will take you outside your comfort zone. It will even require you to do homework.

But this isn't busywork. These lessons give you workable strategies for applying the principles of *The 5 Love Languages of Children.* They offer glimpses of your parenting potential when you speak your children's love languages.

If you're working through this study alone, take heart. Your solo efforts will likely have a profound impact on your relationship with your children. Throughout *The 5 Love Languages of Children*, you'll find accounts of difficult parenting challenges that were overcome by one parent's commitment to learning his or her children's love languages.

If you're working through this study as a couple, let patience, grace, and humor be your companions. Learning a new love language can be difficult, and there's more than a little trial and error involved. Show your appreciation for your spouse's efforts to communicate love in ways that are meaningful to your children, no matter how clumsy those efforts are at first. And be sure to celebrate when those efforts hit the mark.

If you're working through this study in a group, pay attention to what your fellow group members share. Inspiration and wisdom can be found in unexpected places. In your interactions with fellow group members, be generous with your encouragement and sparing with your criticism. Ask appropriate follow-up questions to show your interest in their success. See *The 5 Love Languages of Children* Leader's Guide on pages 106–07 for helpful suggestions in facilitating group discussions.

Regardless of how you approach this study, you should be aware that the lessons in this book will require a significant investment of time and effort. There's a lot of important material in these pages. But it's virtually a risk-free investment. You will see dividends. And the more of yourself you pour into this workbook, the greater your dividends will be.

Enjoy the journey!

GARY CHAPMAN

OBJECTIVE

In reading this chapter, you will learn how unconditional love, communicated through a child's primary love language, lays the groundwork for a healthy, fulfilling parent-child relationship.

LOVE IS THE FOUNDATION

INSTRUCTIONS: Complete this first lesson after reading chapter 1 ("Love Is the Foundation," pp. 15–27) of *The 5 Love Languages of Children*.

KEY TERMS

Primary love language: the love language that most profoundly impacts a person and causes him or her to feel loved.

Love tank: the emotional reservoir inside everyone that is filled when people speak to us in our primary love language.

Unconditional love: a full love that accepts children for who they are, not for what they do.

OPENING QUESTIONS

1. What is the most extravagant expression of love you've ever given your child? Why did you choose that specific way of expressing love? Describe the effort, planning, or financial sacrifice that went into your expression of love.

2. How did your child receive your grand gesture of love? How did you react to your child's response? If you had it to do over again, what would you do differently to make the gesture more meaningful to your child?

THINK ABOUT IT

3. Dr. Chapman and Dr. Campbell begin the chapter with the story of Brad and Emily, who were alerted to their son's need for quality time by his teacher. What red flags have you seen in children—your own or others—that suggested their emotional love tanks weren't getting filled?

4. According to the authors, **"We need to fill our children's emotional tanks with unconditional love, because real love is always unconditional."** What is the difference between conditional love and unconditional love? How does the story of Ana and Sophia emphasize the importance of unconditional love?

5. The authors point out that **"raising emotionally healthy children is an increasingly difficult task these days."** What are some of the factors that make it difficult?

6. Some people fear that showing unconditional love leads to spoiling a child. According to the authors, why is that a misconception? Why do they believe **"no child can receive too much appropriate unconditional love"**?

7. As you move toward the goal of loving your child unconditionally, what realities concerning raising children do you need to keep in mind?

8. What are the two extremes of self-esteem in children? How does each extreme have the potential to damage your child's development?

9. **"Because you want your children to grow into full maturity, you will want to show them love in all the languages and then teach them how to use these for themselves."** What is the lifelong benefit of your child's learning to use all five love languages?

TAKE IT HOME

One way to begin to learn your child's primary love language is to find the common ground you, your spouse, and your child share. The interests, personality traits, and tendencies you have (or don't have) in common can reveal opportunities to show love to your child in meaningful ways (or reveal challenges you face in doing so).

Fill out the Venn diagram below to show your areas of overlap. If you have more than one child, use separate diagrams for each one.

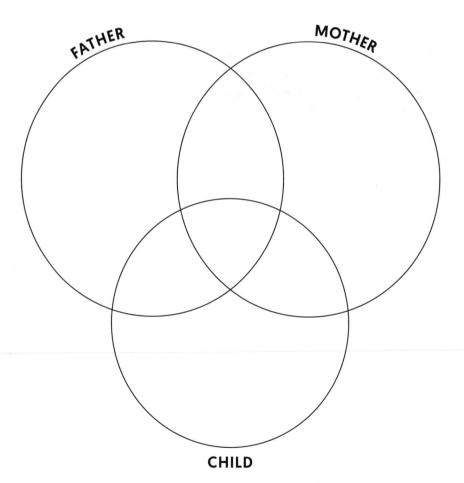

HOW CAN I LOVE YOU? LET ME COUNT THE WAYS

List different ways you can show love to your child in each of the following categories. For example, for physical touch, your list might include everything from a bedtime cuddle to an elaborate high-five/handshake routine. For words of affirmation, you might put down recounting the highlights of your child's performance after a sporting event, or a nighttime ritual of sharing one thing your child did that made you proud that day. For quality time, your list might mention making pancakes together on Saturday mornings or flying kites together at the park. For gifts, you could include anything from an addition to one of your child's collections to a puppy. For acts of service, it might be building a blanket fort or fixing a flat tire on a bike.

PHYSICAL TOUCH	WORDS OF AFFIRMATION

QUALITY TIME	GIFTS

ACTS OF SERVICE	

LOVE CHALLENGE

Have you shown your child conditional love, perhaps without even realizing that you were doing it? Have you, through your words or attitude, given your child the impression that he or she must earn your love? If so, what can you do this week to make things right? How can you make your child feel unconditionally loved?

Use this space for more notes, quotes, or lessons learned from the chapter.

OBJECTIVE

In reading this chapter, you will learn how the purposeful use
of physical touch can fill your child's emotional love tank.

LOVE LANGUAGE #1: PHYSICAL TOUCH

INSTRUCTIONS: Complete this second lesson after reading chapter 2 ("Love Language #1: Physical Touch," pp. 29–42) of *The 5 Love Languages of Children*.

KEY TERM

Physical touch: a love language in which a person experiences emotional wholeness through human contact.

OPENING QUESTIONS

1. What are some of the most meaningful ways you've used physical touch to express love to your child? Why were these moments meaningful to you?

2. When you were a child, how demonstrative were your parents when it came to expressing love through physical touch? How do you explain their attitudes toward physical touch? How much did their attitudes affect your parenting style when it comes to physical expressions of love and affection?

THINK ABOUT IT

3.   Why do the authors say that **"physical touch is the easiest love language to use unconditionally"**?

4.   Research studies have shown the necessity of demonstrating love through physical touch. What is one reason physical touch can have a positive impact on babies? What are the consequences when a baby does not receive love through physical touch?

5.   What circumstances, especially in American culture, deprive infants and toddlers of the touches they need? What happens as a baby grows and becomes more active? What causes parents to scale back their physical affection with boys as they get older?

6.   Why does a hug every morning before school and a hug every afternoon after school have the potential to change your child's entire outlook on the day? What other types of touch are effective with school-age children?

7. The authors remind parents that as their child grows, **"the emotional love tank also grows and keeping it full becomes more difficult."** Why is it essential for parents to work through the difficulties to show love through physical touch to tweens and teens—especially adolescent girls?

8. Based on the authors' explanation and Michelle's description of her son Jaden, what clues can you look for to determine whether physical touch is your child's primary love language?

9. Dr. Chapman and Dr. Campbell conclude the chapter with testimonials from Stella, Jeremy, Hunter, and Taylor. What would you like to hear your child say when they're asked how they know that you love them?

TAKE IT HOME

Parents' use of physical touch with their child can follow many different progressions. Some parents start out offering nearly constant physical touch as they hold, cuddle, and rock their newborn. They then scale back their physical touches for various reasons as their child gets older. Other parents start out tentatively, offering limited physical touches, due perhaps to their insecurities as new parents or fears about their child's frailty. As they become more comfortable, they increase their physical contact.

What about you? What would your history of physical touch with your child look like? On the graph below, chart your progression of showing love and affection through physical touch with your child, from birth to age twelve (or up to his or her current age).

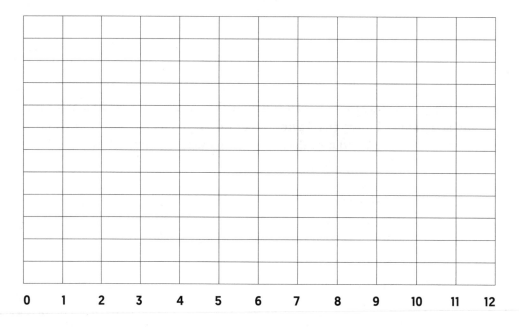

What conclusions can you draw about your use of physical touch with your child based on this graph?

PHYSICAL TOUCH METERS

Place a mark on each of the following lines to indicate how often you use that form of physical touch with your child. Then jot down a few ideas for increasing your use of the physical touches that scored lowest on your meters.

KISSES

Never   Practically Always

_____

HUGS

Never   Practically Always

_____

HIGH FIVES

Never   Practically Always

_____

WRESTLING

Never   Practically Always

_____

CUDDLING

Never   Practically Always

_____

LOVE CHALLENGE

For many parents, the challenge is not learning how to show love through physical touch. Even the most standoffish parents offer occasional hugs, handshakes, or pats on the back. Instead, the challenge is learning how to use frequent physical touch in a purposeful and meaningful way that fills a child's emotional love tank. How will you rise to that challenge this week? What will you do to signal to your child that you're serious about learning to speak the love language of physical touch?

Use this space for more notes, quotes, or lessons learned from the chapter.

OBJECTIVE

In reading this chapter, you will learn how to use words of affirmation
to express love in ways that fill your child's emotional love tank.

LOVE LANGUAGE #2: WORDS OF AFFIRMATION

INSTRUCTIONS: Complete this third lesson after reading chapter 3 ("Love Language #2: Words of Affirmation," pp. 45–59) of *The 5 Love Languages of Children*.

KEY TERM

Words of affirmation: verbal and written expressions of love, appreciation, and encouragement that communicate love in profound ways for people who speak that love language.

OPENING QUESTIONS

1. An ancient proverb says, "The tongue has power over life and death." When was the last time someone said something that made you feel truly alive—words that added a spring to your step or energized your life? Why do you think those words had such an impact on you?

2. When was the last time you said something for the purpose of making someone else's life a little better? How were your words received? How did you know what to say?

THINK ABOUT IT

3. According to the authors, **"Long before they can understand the meanings of words, children receive emotional messages."** How can parents communicate emotional warmth and love at this stage? How can parents help a child associate the words "I love you" with affectionate feelings?

4. The authors point out, **"Once your child begins to understand what your 'I love you' means, you can use these words in different ways and times, so that they become connected to regular events."** How did Kathleen's mother connect genuine praise—the kind that says "I love you"—with a regular event in her household? What were the immediate and long-term results? How can you do something similar for your child?

5. **"Praise and affection are often combined in the messages we give to a child. We need to distinguish the two."** What is the difference between praise and affection? How can parents ensure that their words of praise don't lose their meaning? What happens if you use praise too frequently?

6. The authors write, **"To a young child, almost every experience is new. Learning to walk, to talk, or to ride a bicycle requires constant courage."** Why is it crucial for parents to use the right words in these circumstances? What role do parental encouraging words play in speech development? What role do they play in a child's learning of social skills?

7. Why is the physical, mental, emotional, and spiritual health of parents a key factor in their use of encouraging words? According to the authors, what is the greatest enemy parents face in encouraging their children? What can parents do to influence their child's reaction to what they say?

8. When are encouraging words most effective? What should be the goal of parents who want to offer encouraging words to their child? How do encouraging words offer much-needed guidance for children? The authors offer a stark reminder: **"All children are guided by someone. If you as their parents are not their primary guides, then other influences and individuals assume that role."** Who or what may fill that role in your child's life if you don't?

9. The authors say, **"Too often parents give the right message but in the wrong manner."** Give an example of when you've experienced that personally or witnessed it in the life of someone else. What happens when a positive message is delivered in a negative manner? How can parents prevent their guidance from becoming **"an exercise in prohibition"**?

TAKE IT HOME

How did you respond to words of affirmation when you were a child? Use the chart below to describe three specific instances when words of affirmation made a difference to your younger self.

ONE	
What was said?	
Who said it?	
What were the circumstances?	
Why do you still remember it?	
TWO	
What was said?	
Who said it?	
What were the circumstances?	
Why do you still remember it?	
THREE	
What was said?	
Who said it?	
What were the circumstances?	
Why do you still remember it?	

THE RIGHT WORDS AT THE RIGHT TIME

Any time is a good time for words of affirmation. But certain situations seem to cry out for them. For each of the following situations, come up with some words of affirmation that might be especially meaningful.

Your child didn't make the school basketball team.

You overhear your child comforting her little cousin.

Your child models the new outfit she just got for her birthday.

Your child tries to learn a new skill such as juggling or knitting.

Your child is being ghosted by a friend.

Your child completes a household chore without being asked.

LOVE CHALLENGE

Dr. Chapman and Dr. Cambell suggest keeping a notebook titled "Words of Affirmation" in which you write statements you can use to affirm, praise, and encourage your child. What will be the first statements you write in your notebook this week? For what circumstances or events in your child's life should you prepare words of affirmation?

Use this space for more notes, quotes, or lessons learned from the chapter.

OBJECTIVE

reading this chapter, you will learn how to use quality time and quality conversation to express love in ways that fill your child's love tank.

LOVE LANGUAGE #3: QUALITY TIME

INSTRUCTIONS: Complete this fourth lesson after reading chapter 4 ("Love Language #3: Quality Time," pp. 61–75) of *The 5 Love Languages of Children.*

KEY TERMS

Quality time: a way of expressing love through spending purposeful time with, and directing your full attention to, another person.

Quality conversation: sympathetic dialogue in which two people share their experiences, thoughts, feelings, and desires in a friendly, uninterrupted context.

OPENING QUESTIONS

1. On an average day, how much time do you spend with your child? What would a breakdown of that time spent together look like? For example, how much time do you spend together during meals? Preparing for bedtime? Traveling in the car?

2. How much of the time you spend with your child would you consider to be "quality time"? How do you define quality time? How much of the time you spend together would your child consider to be quality time? How do you think your child would define quality time?

THINK ABOUT IT

3. The scenario Kate shares about her daughter Ella trying to get her attention while she was trying to pay bills is all too familiar for most parents. During what "inconvenient" times does your child tend to compete for your undivided attention? How do you usually respond?

4. The authors acknowledge that **"it takes real effort to carve out this kind of time in your schedule."** Why is it important to think of quality time as an investment in the future? What do you hope the dividends will be from your investment?

5. What is the connection between positive eye contact and unconditional love? What happens when parents refuse to look at their child as a means of punishment?

6. Quality time opens the door to quality conversation. Phil Briggs found that his son opened up to him when the two golfed together. Other parents have discovered that quality conversation can spring from throwing a football or making pasta together. What kind of environment would be most conducive to quality conversation with your child? How can quality conversation benefit your child later in life?

7. **"All children love stories. Reading to them is a great way to begin your bedtime ritual—and do make it a ritual, because this will help to keep communications open when they become teenagers."** How can parents use stories to initiate quality conversation with their child? Why is it important that a parent not become **"a victim of the urgent"** when it comes to bedtime reading rituals?

8. The authors write, **"During the first eight years of a child's life, you can assume a fairly sane schedule, as the child's life centers primarily around the home. But as your child grows and becomes more involved in activities outside the home, you need to spend more time and effort preparing for family quality time. Otherwise it just won't happen."** What three ideas do they offer to help you get started with your preparation?

9. What challenges did Gerry and Maggie face with their schedules? What was their first clue that something wasn't right with their son, Jonathan? What specific steps did Maggie take to speak her son's love language of quality time? What were the results? What are your takeaways from Gerry and Maggie's story?

TAKE IT HOME

Where can you find quality time to spend with your child in your busy schedule? Let's find out. Think about your typical weekly schedule. On the clock faces below, indicate times you can set aside for your child.

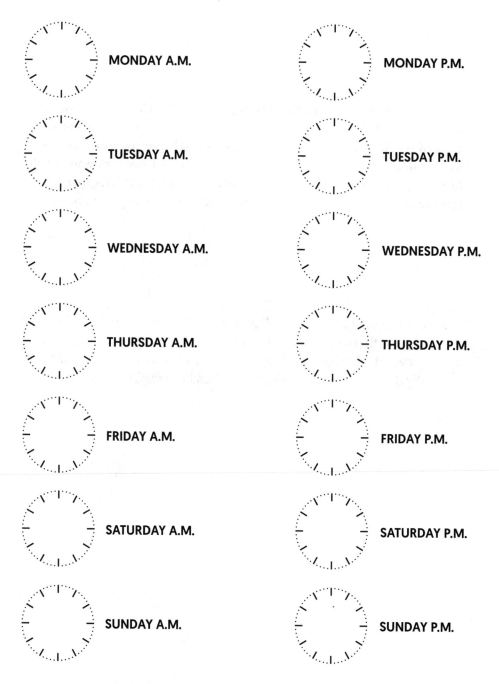

MONDAY A.M.

MONDAY P.M.

TUESDAY A.M.

TUESDAY P.M.

WEDNESDAY A.M.

WEDNESDAY P.M.

THURSDAY A.M.

THURSDAY P.M.

FRIDAY A.M.

FRIDAY P.M.

SATURDAY A.M.

SATURDAY P.M.

SUNDAY A.M.

SUNDAY P.M.

PUTTING THE QUALITY IN QUALITY TIME

Quality time is one of the most challenging—and one of the most rewarding—love languages to master. The first step in overcoming these challenges is to anticipate them. On the chart below, you'll find a few common challenges parents face in showing love to their child through quality time. You'll also find a couple of blank spaces to add others that you've encountered. Next to each challenge, write a few ideas you can use to overcome it.

CHALLENGE	IDEAS
You have a hard time focusing on your child during your time together.	
You're not sure what to do during your time together.	
Your schedule is too unpredictable to schedule time together.	
Your child never seems satisfied with the time you spend together.	

LOVE CHALLENGE

Tomorrow you will have twenty-four hours to spend the way you see fit. What special gesture can you make in those twenty-four hours to signal to your child that you want to prioritize quality time with him or her?

Use this space for more notes, quotes, or lessons learned from the chapter.

OBJECTIVE

In reading this chapter, you will learn how to use well-chosen gifts
to express love in ways that fill your child's emotional love tank.

LOVE LANGUAGE #4: GIFTS

INSTRUCTIONS: Complete this fifth lesson after reading chapter 5 ("Love Language #4: Gifts," pp. 77–89) of *The 5 Love Languages of Children*.

KEY TERM

Receiving gifts: a love language in which a person experiences emotional wholeness through well-chosen presents.

OPENING QUESTIONS

1. If you could give your child one gift, what would it be? Don't limit your thinking to things that are realistically possible for you. For example, if your child still talks about a trip she took to the children's museum, your gift might be a bedroom filled with reminders of her favorite exhibits. If your child is an animal lover, your gift might be opening a sanctuary for rescue dogs and cats. If your child misses a best friend or family member who moved away, your gift might be an entire week to spend with that person.

2. What is the closest version of that gift that you could realistically give your child? For example, you may not be able to arrange a weeklong visit, but you might be able to arrange a special video chat. Or you might put together a scrapbook featuring pictures of your child and her friend or family member.

THINK ABOUT IT

3. If your child were asked the same question that Rachel was asked—"Why are you so sure that your parents love you?"—how do you think your child would respond? What items could he or she point to as "evidence" of your love?

4. Based on the story Julie told about her daughters, Mallory and Meredith, what clues would you look for to determine whether gifts is your child's primary love language? If it is your child's primary love language, why is it important to use a combination of the other four love languages as well?

5. The authors emphasize, **"A true gift is not payment for services rendered; rather, it is an expression of love for the individual and is freely given by the donor."** Why does that distinction need to be made in parental giving to children?

6. One of the great things about having a child whose primary love language is gifts is that you can expand your thinking about what constitutes a gift. The authors point out that even necessities can be given as gifts. What can parents do to transform a necessity into a meaningful gift?

7. What warning does Dr. Chapman give about buying toys as gifts? Why is it important to be very selective? What questions should parents ask themselves before they make a toy purchase?

8. If parents aren't careful, how can gifts become substitutes for the other love languages? Why is the abuse of gift-giving especially common among noncustodial parents after a divorce? What happens to children who receive these ill-advised gifts?

9. What are the guidelines for giving that the authors recommend for parents of children whose primary love language is gifts?

TAKE IT HOME

Learning to give meaningful gifts involves some trial and error. Not every gift will get the same reaction. You can narrow down your child's specific preferences by keeping track of how he or she reacted to past gifts. Think of things, big and small, that you've given your child and put them in the appropriate column below, based on your child's response to it.

YAY! My child loved it.	MEH. My child thought it was okay.	NO THANKS. My child was underwhelmed.

What patterns do you see in these lists? What can you tell about your child's gift preferences?

THE RIGHT GIFT FOR THE OCCASION

One of the most powerful ways to show love to a child whose primary love language is gifts is to find just the right present for certain occasions. Below you'll find a list of occasions. Think of a creative gift for each one. For example, for a long car ride, you might put together a travel pack—a backpack filled with a coloring book, crayons, snacks, puzzles, and other items to help your child pass the time.

THE OCCASION	THE RIGHT GIFT
Your child prepares for the first day of school.	
Your child has an illness or injury.	
You return home from a business trip.	
Your family plans a long car ride.	
Your child's report card shows significant improvement.	
Your child doesn't make the travel soccer team.	
Your child performs in a music recital.	

LOVE CHALLENGE

In questions 1 and 2 of this lesson, you imagined the ideal gift for your child and the closest approximation to that ideal gift that you could think of. What steps will you take this week to make that approximation happen and prepare to give a memorable gift to your child?

STEP 1

STEP 2

STEP 3

STEP 4

STEP 5

STEP 6

Use this space for more notes, quotes, or lessons learned from the chapter.

OBJECTIVE

In reading this chapter, you will learn how to perform tasks
and complete projects in ways that fill your child's love tank.

LOVE LANGUAGE #5: ACTS OF SERVICE

INSTRUCTIONS: Complete this sixth lesson after reading chapter 6 ("Love Language #5: Acts of Service," pp. 91–106) of *The 5 Love Languages of Children*.

KEY TERM

Acts of service: a love language in which a person experiences emotional wholeness when chores or tasks are done for his or her benefit.

OPENING QUESTIONS

1. Who taught you what serving others looks like? What kind of example did the person set? How have you incorporated those lessons into your own life?

2. How are chores and household responsibilities assigned in your home? Do you think the division of labor is fair? Would everyone else in your household agree? Are there certain chores no one likes doing? If so, which ones? Are there certain chores your child specifically dislikes? If so, which ones? Why?

THINK ABOUT IT

3. The authors make a rather surprising statement: **"As parents, we serve our children—but our primary motivation is not to please them."** What is the chief purpose of parents when it comes to serving our children? How is that different from trying to please them?

4. **"Loving service is not labor."** Why is that important for parents to remember? What is the difference between loving service and labor? Why is it a good idea for parents to do periodic attitude checks when attempting to perform acts of service?

5. What is the ultimate purpose of acts of service to a child? How can the natural self-centeredness of a child get in the way of that purpose? How can parents move them to that ultimate purpose?

6. What impact does conditional love have on parental acts of service, as far as a child is concerned?

7. Why is hospitality an especially powerful way to teach your child by example to show concern for others? What might hospitality look like in your home?

8. The authors say that when a child **"asks you to fix a bicycle or mend a doll's dress, he or she does not merely want to get a task done; your child is crying for emotional love."** What happens when parents recognize and respond to these requests and help with a loving and positive attitude? What happens when parents refuse to respond to the needs or do so with harsh or critical words?

9. Isabella, Bradley, Jodi, and Melania offer a powerful testimony about the impact parental acts of service can have on children. What would you like your child to say about you?

TAKE IT HOME

Rank the following ideas for becoming fluent in acts of service from one to five, according to how feasible they are for you (one would be the easiest for you to put into practice; five would be the most difficult). For each one, write some ideas as to how you could make it work.

_____ Plan to get up a half hour earlier or stay up a half hour later every day to help your child practice something.

_____ Teach your child to cook by making dinner together—and cleaning the kitchen afterward—at least one night a week.

_____ Plan a weekly act of service you and your child can work on together. For example, the two of you might volunteer to collect clothes for the homeless or work at an animal rescue shelter.

_____ Prepare lunch for your child every morning before school. Take time to add a personal touch, whether it's drawing a face on a banana or writing a quick note of encouragement and affection on a napkin.

_____ Prepare flash cards or sample tests to help your child prepare for school exams.

HOW MUCH WOULD IT MEAN?

Below you'll find a list of acts of service. Rate each one on a scale of one to ten, based on how meaningful you think it would be to your child (with one being "not meaningful at all" and ten being "extremely meaningful"). We've left two slots blank for you to fill in with ideas that are specific to your family. After you've rated them all, talk to your child about them. Get his or her reaction. Compare your numbers and talk about areas where there are notable discrepancies.

ACT OF SERVICE	YOU	CHILD
Helping your child with homework		
Serving in a food pantry together		
Organizing your child's messy room		
Repairing your child's bicycle		
Mowing a lawn, raking leaves, or shoveling snow together for an elderly neighbor		
Preparing your child's favorite meal		
Providing special care for your child when he or she is sick		
Making a costume for your child for Halloween or a school project		
Visiting a retirement home together		
Fixing your child's broken toy		
Making your child's lunch and organizing his or her backpack before school		

LOVE CHALLENGE

Is there something that you've been meaning to do for your child but never seem to have the time (or energy or motivation) to tackle it? Perhaps it's a task that gets grandfathered onto every mental to-do list but never gets crossed off. It's likely something your child has given up hope of ever seeing completed. Finishing that task would be a great way of announcing your intention to learn your child's love language. What steps do you need to take this week to complete that task and cross it off your to-do list?

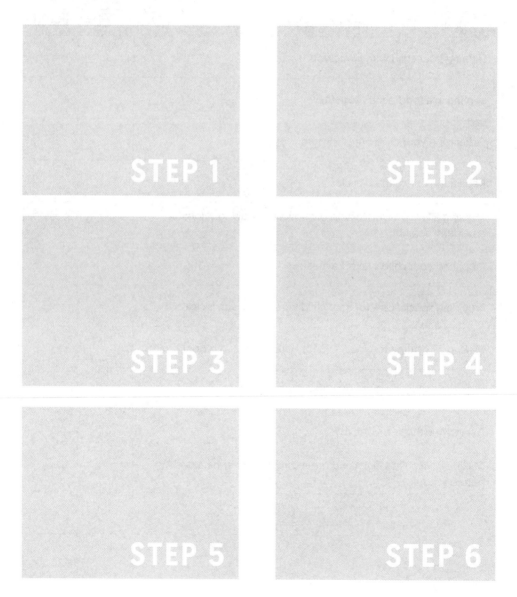

STEP 1

STEP 2

STEP 3

STEP 4

STEP 5

STEP 6

Use this space for more notes, quotes, or lessons learned from the chapter.

OBJECTIVE

In reading this chapter, you will learn how to spot clues to your child's primary
love language so that you can work smarter in making your child feel truly loved.

HOW TO DISCOVER YOUR CHILD'S PRIMARY LOVE LANGUAGE

INSTRUCTIONS: Complete this seventh lesson after reading chapter 7 ("How to Discover Your Child's Primary Love Language," pp. 109–122) of *The 5 Love Languages of Children*.

> **KEY TERM**
>
> **Multilingual:** able to speak all five love languages.

OPENING QUESTIONS

1. What aspects of your child's personality are set? In other words, what traits do you see in your child now that will likely carry over into adulthood?

2. What aspects of your child's personality are still in transition? In what areas do you see your child experimenting with different characteristics, traits, and preferences?

THINK ABOUT IT

3. According to the authors, **"All children are selfish, so they are often unaware of the importance of communicating in ways that are not familiar or comfortable."** Give some examples of when you've noticed this in your child or in other children. What happens when parents learn to speak love languages that are different from our own?

4. Learning a child's primary love language takes time and strategies that differ, depending on the age of the child. What approach should parents take with an infant? How should their approach change as the child gets older? Why is it a mistake to make too many assumptions about a child's primary love language when a child is still young?

5. The authors write, **"As you begin to look for a child's primary love language, it is better not to discuss your search with your children, and especially with teenagers."** Why should you conduct your search without your child knowing what you're doing? What are the five methods the authors recommend for discovering your child's love language?

6. The authors emphasize the importance of using choices to discover a child's love language. How do you keep the choices age-appropriate? What is the difference between the choices you offer a six-year-old and the choices you offer a ten-year-old or fifteen-year-old?

7. What would the fifteen-week experiment look like with your child? Which love language would you start with? Why? Which love language would present the biggest challenge for you? Why? Why is it important to take a week off between love languages? What kind of responses would you look for in your child?

8. According to the authors, **"Teenagers, at times, make it difficult for you to fill their emotional love tank. They are testing you, to see if you really love them."** What kind of behaviors do they use to test you? How can you pass the test? Which love language is your teenager most likely to receive well in this stage?

9. Why is it important to speak all five love languages when a child has only one primary one?

TAKE IT HOME

At the beginning of this chapter in the book, the authors write, **"Spotting your child's primary language of love may take time, but there are clues all around. This is our detective chapter, in which we help you discover your child's primary love language."** Think of this sheet as your detective's notebook. As you investigate your child's primary love language, record your observations here.

Observe how your child expresses love to you and others. What do you notice?

Listen to what your child requests and complains about most often. What patterns do you see?

Offer choices between two love languages. What results do you get?

Try different types of physical touch with your child, everything from hugs to high fives to playful dances together. How does your child respond to your physical touch?

Offer frequent words of affirmation to your child. Focus on several different aspects of your child's personality and behavior. How does your child respond to your words of affirmation?

Set aside blocks of uninterrupted time to spend with your child. This might involve anything from going shopping together to kicking a soccer ball around. How does your child respond to spending quality time with you?

Give your child a few gifts that appeal to his or her specific interests—anything from an item your child collects to a new fish for his or her aquarium. How does your child respond to the gifts?

Perform a few acts of service for your child. Depending on your child's age, this might include anything from organizing a room or closet to creating a study guide for a midterm exam. How does your child respond to your acts of service?

GAME PLAN

I believe my child's primary love language is _____.

The most helpful clues in figuring this out were . . .

Becoming fluent in this love language will be a great opportunity/challenge (circle one) for me because . . .

Here are three steps I will take to begin to speak this love language to my child on a regular basis:

1.

2.

3.

LOVE CHALLENGE

If you haven't yet begun to investigate your child's primary love language, what steps can you take to start this week? How will you incorporate each of the five love languages in your interaction with your child this week? How will you explain what you're doing if your child asks?

STEP 1

STEP 2

STEP 3

STEP 4

STEP 5

STEP 6

Use this space for more notes, quotes, or lessons learned from the chapter.

OBJECTIVE

In reading this chapter, you will learn how you can incorporate your child's love language into your discipline as you work to correct your child's behavior.

DISCIPLINE AND THE LOVE LANGUAGES

INSTRUCTIONS: Complete this eighth lesson after reading chapter 8 ("Discipline and the Love Languages," pp. 125–143) of *The 5 Love Languages of Children*.

KEY TERM

Discipline: the process of establishing parental authority, developing guidelines for a child's behavior, and helping the child live by those guidelines, with the goal to help the child reach a level of maturity that allows him or her to function responsibly in society.

OPENING QUESTIONS

1. What did discipline look like in your home when you were growing up? Did it skew more toward a positive approach, with your parents modeling and teaching right behavior, or a negative approach, with your parents punishing wrong behavior? Explain.

2. What lessons did you take away from your parents' style of discipline? How closely does your discipline of your children resemble your parents' discipline of you? Explain.

THINK ABOUT IT

3. **"Parents play the most important role in the discipline of their children because it is they who interpret to their offspring their culture's generally accepted standards."** This quote from the authors emphasizes the training aspect of discipline—the process of guiding children who have zero knowledge of what the world expects of them to a full understanding. How does this perspective affect the way you approach discipline at various stages of your child's life?

4. The authors write that **"the more a child feels loved, the easier it is to discipline that child."** Why must love always be the guiding force of discipline? What do the authors say to parents who think a child should try to earn their love and affection through good behavior?

5. What two questions do parents need to ask to be able to effectively discipline their child in love? What do parents need to understand about how a child loves? What happens when parents overlook their child's needs when they decide on discipline?

6. How should a child's remorse affect the parents' efforts to discipline the child? What is the connection between guilt and a healthy conscience? What happens when you punish a child who already feels genuinely guilty for his or her behavior?

7. What three nonverbal messages do you send to your child when you make requests? The authors point out, **"A child who is raised in this way comes to feel that he is in partnership with his parents in the molding of his character."** How do the authors respond to those who claim that making requests is too permissive?

8. The authors say that **"commands are a negative means of control because they require harsher tones than requests."** What reactions do commands usually trigger in a child? Why should you use commands sparingly with your child?

9. What are the four essential principles that Dr. Chapman says must guide punishment? Why must you always be aware of fairness when you issue punishment? What happens if you use punishment as your primary form of discipline?

TAKE IT HOME

Dr. Chapman and Dr. Campbell offer five ideas for controlling your child's behavior. How well are you incorporating each one into your parental discipline strategy? For each idea, answer two questions: "What are you doing right?" and "Where can you improve?" For example, when it comes to behavior modification, you may find that your negative reinforcement of withdrawing gaming privileges is especially effective. On the other hand, when it comes to issuing commands, you may find that your child doesn't always respect your authority.

	WHAT ARE YOU DOING RIGHT?	WHERE CAN YOU IMPROVE?
Making requests		
Issuing commands		
Gentle physical manipulations		
Punishment		
Behavior modification		

AVOIDING THE PUNISHMENT TRAP

The authors write, **"As difficult as it may be for you to decide when and how punishment should be used, you must still be prepared to use it and to use it appropriately. This can be facilitated by planning ahead so that you can avoid the 'punishment trap.' This means sitting down with a spouse or good friend to decide appropriate punishment for various offenses. Such planning will keep your anger in check when your child does something that upsets you."**

With that in mind, here are a few offenses your child might commit (along with a couple of blank spaces for you to add your own). Come up with an appropriate punishment for each one. Make your responses as detailed as possible, so that you can refer to them if the need arises.

OFFENSE	PUNISHMENT
Lying to you	
Not completing an important homework assignment	
Fighting with a sibling	
Getting in trouble at school	

LOVE CHALLENGE

Correcting a child's behavior through discipline is one of the toughest challenges that parents face. To strike the right balance between positive and negative methods of control, parents must frequently assess their approach to discipline. How will you broach that subject this week with your spouse? What questions do the two of you need to answer?

Use this space for more notes, quotes, or lessons learned from the chapter.

OBJECTIVE

In reading this chapter, you will learn how to create the kind
of supportive environment and nurture the kind of loving
relationship that motivates your child to learn.

LEARNING AND THE LOVE LANGUAGES

INSTRUCTIONS: Complete this ninth lesson after reading chapter 9 ("Learning and the Love Languages," pp. 145–156) of *The 5 Love Languages of Children*.

KEY TERM

Sensory stimulation: the strategic use of the five senses to boost a child's natural desire to learn.

Emotional maturity: the ability to control anxiety, withstand stress, and maintain balance during times of change that is essential to a child's ability to learn.

OPENING QUESTIONS

1. What kind of student were you in school? Did good grades come easily to you, or did you struggle to get Cs? How do you explain that? Who or what shaped your attitude toward learning? Describe that influence.

2. When it comes to learning and school, in what areas would you like your child to follow your example? In what areas would you like to see your child forge a different path from the one you took?

THINK ABOUT IT

3.   The authors write that **"small children love to learn. They are born with an innate hunger for learning that remains strong."** How might parents negatively impact their child's love and hunger for learning without realizing it? Give an example of how that might occur.

4.   **"Children are more emotional than cognitive—that is, they remember feelings more readily than they do facts."** What does this mean for parents who take an active role in their child's development by reading stories or looking for teachable moments?

5.   According to the authors, **"As the child grows, his ability to learn increases because of several factors, the most important of which is his emotional maturity."** How can parents foster emotional growth in their child?

6.   The authors remind parents that **"studies consistently show that parental involvement in education helps children thrive in school."** Parents have a great advantage over people outside the family because they know and understand their child. Based on what you know about your child, what forms should your involvement take? Explain.

7. Not only does anxiety cause emotional upheaval in a child, but it also interferes with learning development. According to the authors, what happens if a child **"is distressed with anxiety or melancholy, or feels unloved"**? When does learning-related anxiety often appear among children? What role does emotional maturity play in a child's ability to weather the transition from concrete to abstract thinking?

8. What is the key to motivating a child? What are three things parents can do to help their child stay motivated?

9. The authors apply the concept of taking responsibility to the familiar scenario of completing homework. What would a typical homework struggle look like in your household? What would be your best strategy for encouraging your child to take responsibility for homework?

TAKE IT HOME

According to the authors, **"Children discover life through the five senses. A home environment that is rich in stimulation of vision, hearing, touch, taste, and smell will feed their natural desire to discover and learn."**

How would you rate your home environment in each of those five areas in terms of how stimulating it is to your child's learning process? Mark each of the lines below to indicate your answer and then list some examples of how you help stimulate that sense in your child. For example, reading picture books stimulates vision; playing musical instruments stimulates hearing; fingerpainting stimulates touch; comparing sweet and sour fruits stimulates taste; and using scented Play-Doh stimulates smell.

VISION

Not very stimulating at all   Extremely stimulating

Examples:

HEARING

Not very stimulating at all   Extremely stimulating

Examples:

TOUCH

Not very stimulating at all   Extremely stimulating

Examples:

TASTE

Not very stimulating at all   Extremely stimulating

Examples:

SMELL

Not very stimulating at all   Extremely stimulating

Examples:

BE AN ENCOURAGER

The authors point out that one thing parents can do to motivate their child is to encourage the child's interests. Create a pie chart in the circle below to represent your child's interests right now. The biggest wedges will represent the things that occupy most of your child's time and attention these days. The smaller wedges will represent occasional, more minor interests.

Which of your child's current interests is most interesting to you? Explain.

List three things you can do to encourage that interest.

1.

2.

3.

How can you encourage that interest without taking away the initiative from your child?

LOVE CHALLENGE

Dr. Chapman and Dr. Campbell conclude chapter 9 with the story of Kelly and her daughter Julia. Kelly discovered that speaking Julia's love language, acts of service, during the crucial few minutes before and after school made a huge difference in Julia's attitude and motivation. With that in mind, what's one thing you can do this week to speak your child's love language during a crucial part of the day?

Use this space for more notes, quotes, or lessons learned from the chapter.

OBJECTIVE

In reading this chapter, you will learn how to manage your child's anger by keeping your child's emotional tank full and by guiding him or her from negative expressions of anger to positive ones.

ANGER AND LOVE

INSTRUCTIONS: Complete this tenth lesson after reading chapter 10 ("Anger and Love," pp. 159–175) of *The 5 Love Languages of Children*.

KEY TERM

Passive-aggressive behavior: a common and destructive way to handle anger that gets back at a person indirectly; a subconscious determination to do exactly the opposite of what an authority figure wants.

OPENING QUESTIONS

1. How do you usually express your anger? How do your loved ones typically react when you express anger? If you could change one thing about the way you respond when you're angry, what would it be?

2. What similarities or differences do you see among the way you express anger, the way your spouse expresses anger, and the way your child expresses anger?

THINK ABOUT IT

3. The authors suggest that **"anger more commonly creates problems than solves them."** What can happen when anger is not expressed for righteous reasons?

4. **"Few adults have mastered appropriate ways to handle anger. One reason is that most anger is expressed subconsciously, below the level of our awareness. Another is that few adults have made the transition from immature to mature means of dealing with anger."** To back up this claim, the authors present two scenarios involving the Jackson family. What do the parents do in the second scenario to create a more positive outcome?

5. The authors point out that anger **"can have beneficial results, if it energizes and motivates us to take action when we would otherwise remain silent."** Give an example from your own experience of how anger, properly managed, led to a positive result.

6. Passive-aggressive behavior is one of the most common and destructive ways children handle anger. What three clues do the authors offer to help you to determine whether your child's behavior is passive-aggressive? How can you distinguish between harmless and harmful passive-aggressive behavior?

7. How does speaking your child's love language at an early age help prevent passive-aggressive behavior later?

8. Why are patience and wisdom essential in helping your child climb the "Anger Ladder"? What is the biggest challenge you anticipate as you help your child climb it? Explain.

9. Why do the authors say, **"If you want to train your children to manage anger in a mature fashion, you must *allow them to express it verbally, as unpleasant as that may be*"**? What are three things you can do to "seize the moment" after your child has verbally expressed anger?

TAKE IT HOME

One of the challenges in helping your child manage anger is managing your own anger. Passive-aggressive behavior has a way of triggering the worst impulses in parents. Our first reaction is often to lash out, to respond in kind, to demand respect, or to punish an angry outburst. If, however, we resist those initial impulses and take a moment to consider the big picture of anger management, we will find a better way to respond.

For each of the following scenarios, write what your first, unfiltered reaction likely would be. Then come up with a better, more positive reaction to the situation, one that will help your child learn to manage anger.

YOUR CHILD DOES THIS	YOUR FIRST REACTION IS TO	A BETTER RESPONSE WOULD BE
Throws a tantrum		
Won't keep his room clean		
Lies to you		
Puts zero effort into homework		
Gets in trouble at school		

ANGER MANAGEMENT LAND

Here's a fun way to map out the path of anger management for your child. Follow the instructions to get from the start to the finish.

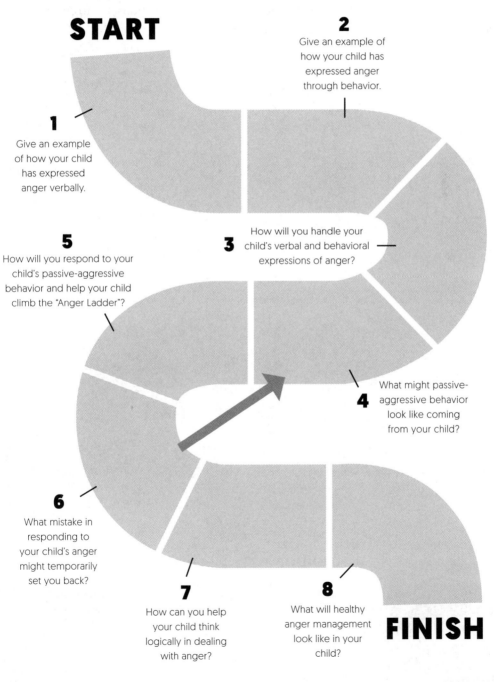

START

1
Give an example of how your child has expressed anger verbally.

2
Give an example of how your child has expressed anger through behavior.

3
How will you handle your child's verbal and behavioral expressions of anger?

4
What might passive-aggressive behavior look like coming from your child?

5
How will you respond to your child's passive-aggressive behavior and help your child climb the "Anger Ladder"?

6
What mistake in responding to your child's anger might temporarily set you back?

7
How can you help your child think logically in dealing with anger?

8
What will healthy anger management look like in your child?

FINISH

LOVE CHALLENGE

Not everyone responds to anger in a healthy way 100 percent of the time. Chances are, you have at least a few past angry outbursts that you regret, perhaps even one directed at your child. You can set a powerful example to your child by apologizing for it. What will you say this week to your child—or to your spouse, in front of your child—to make amends for your mishandled anger?

Use this space for more notes, quotes, or lessons learned from the chapter.

OBJECTIVE

In reading this chapter, you will learn how to work through the challenges of
being a single parent so that you can keep your child's emotional tank full.

SPEAKING THE LOVE LANGUAGES IN SINGLE-PARENT FAMILIES

INSTRUCTIONS: Complete this eleventh lesson after reading chapter 11 ("Speaking the Love Languages in Single-Parent Families," pp. 177–189) of *The 5 Love Languages of Children*.

KEY TERM

Bargaining: the stage of grief in which a child who has lost a parent to death or divorce refuses to accept the reality of the situation and attempts to manipulate one or both parents.

OPENING QUESTIONS

1. Think of the single parents you know—friends, loved ones, coworkers, neighbors, and acquaintances who are either divorced, widowed, or never married. What characteristics do they have in common that set them apart from married people or childless single people? What realities do single parents face that married people and childless single people don't have to consider?

2. Think of the children from single-parent homes that you know—kids who grew up without regular contact with one of their parents. What characteristics do they have in common?

THINK ABOUT IT

3. Addressing single parents, the authors write, **"You know all too well the time pressures, the economic demands, and the social and personal changes you and your children have experienced."** What specific challenges do single parents face that married parents don't when it comes to meeting the emotional needs of their child?

4. Why is divorce, especially when it's not handled well by the two parents, particularly traumatic for children? What kind of emotional damage do single custodial parents have to deal with in their children in the wake of a divorce?

5. The authors point out that the most common emotions of children of divorce and those whose parent has died are fear, anger, and anxiety. Research shows that these feelings still frequently surface a decade or more after the divorce. The authors go on to say, **"Such feelings can readily drain love from a child's emotional tank"** as they go through the stages of grief. What can help them move through those stages more quickly?

6. The authors say, **"Children who are overwhelmed with negative feelings have a hard time thinking clearly."** Why is reading a useful strategy for the single parents of those children? What kind of stories and books should you look for? How can you make your reading time more interactive?

7. Why is it important for a single parent to take the initiative in asking for help? Where can you find necessary resources? How can you get past any reluctance you may have in making your needs known?

8. The authors explain the stark reality facing a child of divorce this way: **"A child's need for emotional love is just as important after the divorce as it was before. The difference is that the child's love tank has been ruptured by the severe trauma of divorce."** How can a parent repair the child's love tank?

9. The authors take a quick break from discussing the needs of children of divorce to offer an important reminder: **"A single parent's emotional need for love is just as real as anyone else's need."** It's hard to fill your child's love tank if your own love tank is almost empty. What can you do to start to fill your own love tank after your divorce or death of your spouse?

TAKE IT HOME

One of the most difficult challenges widowed or divorced single parents—and the people who love them—face is helping their child work through the stages of grief brought on by the divorce or death. The authors identify four such stages (two of which are anger). The following questions are designed to help you create a strategy for working through each stage with your child.

DENIAL
How can you help your child accept the reality of your loss?

How can you and your child work together to create a "new normal" for your family in the wake of your loss—one built around your child's primary love language?

How will your "new normal" account for the feelings of sadness, loss, and rejection that your child experiences?

ANGER—AND MORE ANGER
How will you react when your child blames you for the divorce or death of a parent and directs their anger at you?

How will you react when your child blames your ex? Or God?

How will you react when your child doesn't express the anger he or she is clearly feeling?

BARGAINING
How will you react to your child's efforts to reunite you with your ex?

How will you respond if your child resorts to radical misbehavior to get your attention (or the attention of your ex)?

How will you convince your child of your constant concern for his or her well-being?

BUILDING A SUPPORT TEAM

The authors emphasize that **"no parent can single-handedly meet a child's need for love."** You need help. You need a team of people who care about you and your child—a support group you trust. No one can assemble that team for you because you have the final say on who you will allow to influence your child. Listed below, you'll find some possibilities to consider. (Add your own ideas in the blank spaces.) On a scale of one to ten, rate how feasible or advisable it would be to enlist each for your support team. Write a brief explanation for each rating, along with any ideas for making that person a more feasible helper.

PERSON	RATING	COMMENT
Parent(s)		
Sibling(s)		
Grandparent(s)		
Aunt(s)/Uncle(s)/ Cousin(s)		
Friend(s)		
Coworker(s)		
Neighbor(s)		
Pastor/Spiritual Leader(s)		
Your Ex-in-Law(s)		

LOVE CHALLENGE

If you're a single parent, what can you do this week to meet your own need for love and companionship? What would make a difference in your life right now? Who can you reach out to for company and conversation? If you're not a single parent, but you know one, what can you do this week to show love and companionship to that person?

Use this space for more notes, quotes, or lessons learned from the chapter.

OBJECTIVE

In reading this chapter, you will learn how becoming fluent in
your spouse's primary love language helps you "work smarter"
in showing love in a meaningful way.

SPEAKING THE LOVE LANGUAGES IN MARRIAGE

INSTRUCTIONS: Complete this twelfth lesson after reading chapter 12 ("Speaking the Love Languages in Marriage," pp. 191–204) of *The 5 Love Languages of Children*.

KEY TERM

In-love experience: a euphoric emotional obsession in which a person fixates on the positive aspects of a romantic partner—and of the relationship—but loses sight of practical realities.

OPENING QUESTIONS

1. What are some subtle things you notice about your spouse that other people might miss? What are some things about your spouse that are still complete mysteries to you, even after all the time you've been together?

2. Understanding love languages involves celebrating our differences. In what ways are you and your spouse similar? In what ways are you different? Do your similarities outnumber your differences, or vice versa? Which similarities are most important? Which differences present the biggest challenge?

THINK ABOUT IT

3. According to the authors, what are two common mistakes spouses make in their assumptions about love languages?

4. Where do you see the biggest opportunities to make your spouse feel loved by using words of affirmation? What challenges will you face in incorporating words of affirmation into your daily routine? How can you make sure that your words of affirmation are effective in making your spouse feel loved?

5. Where do you see the biggest opportunities to make your spouse feel loved by giving him or her quality time? What challenges will you face in incorporating quality time into your daily routine? How can you make sure that your efforts to give quality time are effective in making your spouse feel loved?

6. Where do you see the biggest opportunities to make your spouse feel loved by giving gifts? What challenges will you face in incorporating gift-giving into your daily routine? How can you make sure that your efforts to give gifts are effective in making your spouse feel loved?

7. Where do you see the biggest opportunities to make your spouse feel loved by performing acts of service? What challenges will you face in incorporating acts of service into your daily routine? How can you make sure that your acts of service are effective in making your spouse feel loved?

8. Where do you see the biggest opportunities to make your spouse feel loved through physical touch? What challenges will you face in incorporating purposeful physical touch into your daily routine? How can you make sure that your physical touches are effective in making your spouse feel loved?

9. Based on conversations with your spouse, things you've read in *The 5 Love Languages of Children*, and your own observations, what do you think is your spouse's primary love language? Explain. What happens when you and your spouse speak each other's primary love language regularly?

TAKE IT HOME

One of the biggest challenges married couples face is the language gap that results from their speaking two different love languages. The first step in closing that gap is acknowledging the challenges it creates. Use the following questions to explore the language gap between you and your spouse.

My primary love language is _____.

My natural instinct is to show love to my spouse by doing things like . . .

When I tried those things in the past, the response I got was . . .

I've discovered that my spouse's primary love language is _____.

The biggest challenge in learning this language is . . .

Now I try to show love to my spouse by doing things like . . .

And the response I get is . . .

LOVE LANGUAGE TAKEAWAYS

Regardless of your spouse's primary love language, it's wise to be conversant in all five love languages. Here's a chance to summarize the key information for each one.

WORDS OF AFFIRMATION

Mistake to Avoid

Key Detail to Remember

Idea That Would Appeal Especially to Your Spouse

QUALITY TIME

Mistake to Avoid

Key Detail to Remember

Idea That Would Appeal Especially to Your Spouse

GIFTS

Mistake to Avoid

Key Detail to Remember

Idea That Would Appeal Especially to Your Spouse

ACTS OF SERVICE

Mistake to Avoid

Key Detail to Remember

Idea That Would Appeal Especially to Your Spouse

PHYSICAL TOUCH

Mistake to Avoid

Key Detail to Remember

Idea That Would Appeal Especially to Your Spouse

Additional notes

LOVE CHALLENGE

Are you 100 percent sure that you know your spouse's primary love language? Have you talked to your spouse about it? Have you asked your spouse which expressions of love have had the biggest impact on him or her? Have you talked about what, specifically, your spouse would like most from you? If the answer to any of those questions is no, how will you start a fact-finding conversation with your spouse this week?

Use this space for more notes, quotes, or lessons learned from the chapter.

THE 5 LOVE LANGUAGES OF CHILDREN LEADER'S GUIDE

Congratulations! You're on the cusp of an exciting adventure. You're about to lead a small group through twelve studies that will enrich relationships and change lives. And you'll have a front-row seat to it all.

You'll find that every small group presents its own unique challenges and opportunities. But there are some tips that can help you get the most out of any small-group study, whether you're a seasoned veteran or a first-time leader.

1. Communicate.

From the outset, you'll want to give members a sense of how your group dynamic will work. To maximize your time together, group members will need to read each lesson's assigned chapter of *The 5 Love Languages of Children* and then complete the "Opening Questions" (questions 1–2) and "Think About It" section (questions 3–9) *before* the meeting. The "Take It Home" and "Love Challenge" activities should be completed after the meeting.

2. Keep a good pace.

Your first meeting will begin with introductions (if necessary). After that, you'll ask group members to share their responses to the first two "Getting Started" questions. These are icebreakers. Their purpose is merely to introduce the session topic. You'll want to give everyone a chance to share, but you don't want to get sidetracked by overly long discussions here.

The "Think About It" section (questions 3–9) is the heart of the study. This is where most of your discussion should occur. You'll need to establish a good pace, making sure that you give each question its due while allowing enough time to tackle all of them. After you've finished your discussion of the questions, briefly go over the "Take It Home" and "Love Challenge" sections so that group members know what their "homework" will be.

Your next meeting will begin with a brief review of that homework. Ask volunteers to share their responses to the "Take It Home" activities and their experiences in implementing the "Love Challenge." After about five minutes of reviewing your group members' application of the previous lesson, begin your new lesson.

3. Prepare.
Read each chapter, answer the study questions, and work through the take-home material, just like your group members will do. Try to anticipate questions or comments your group members will have. If you have time, think of stories from your own parenting experience or from the experiences of people you know that apply to the lesson. That way, if you have a lull during your study, you can use the stories to spark conversation.

4. Be open and vulnerable.
Not everyone is comfortable with sharing the details of their parenting experience with other people. Yet openness and vulnerability are essential in a group setting. That's where you come in. If you have the courage to be vulnerable, to share less-than-flattering details about your own experience, you may give others the courage to do the same.

5. Emphasize and celebrate the uniqueness of every parent.
Some group members may feel intimidated by other people's seemingly successful parenting. Others may find that strategies for learning love languages that work for some people don't work for them—and they may get discouraged. You can head off that discouragement by opening up about your own struggles and successes. Help group members see that, beneath the surface, every parent faces challenges.

6. Create a safe haven where people feel free—and comfortable—to share.
Ask group members to agree to some guidelines before your first meeting. For example, what is said in the group setting stays in the group setting. And every person's voice deserves to be heard. If you find that some group members are quick to give unsolicited advice or criticism when other people share, remind the group that every parenting situation is unique. What works for one may not work for another. If the problem persists, talk with your advice givers and critics one-on-one. Help them see how their well-intended comments may be having the unintended effect of discouraging others from talking.

7. Follow up.
The questions and activities in this book encourage group members to incorporate new strategies with their children and make significant changes to their parenting routines. You can be the cheerleader your group members need by celebrating their successes and congratulating them for their courage and commitment. Also, by checking in each week with your group members, you create accountability and give them motivation to apply *The 5 Love Languages of Children* principles to their parenting.

Help children discover their love language using this illustrated hardcover book.

Gary Chapman and Rick Osborne help children learn about the importance of love in this wonderfully imaginative and classically illustrated children's hardcover book featuring four-color illustrations (with hidden details!) by Wilson Williams, Jr., and based on Gary's bestselling *The 5 Love Languages*. FREE mobile app available.

Also available as an eBook

Simple ways to strengthen relationships.

- TAKE THE LOVE LANGUAGE® QUIZ

- DOWNLOAD FREE RESOURCES AND STUDY GUIDES

- BROWSE THE LOVE LANGUAGE® GIFT GUIDE

- SUBSCRIBE TO PODCASTS

- SHOP THE STORE

- SIGN UP FOR THE NEWSLETTER

Visit www.5lovelanguages.com

CONNECT WITH YOUR FAMILY WITHOUT BREAKING THE BANK.

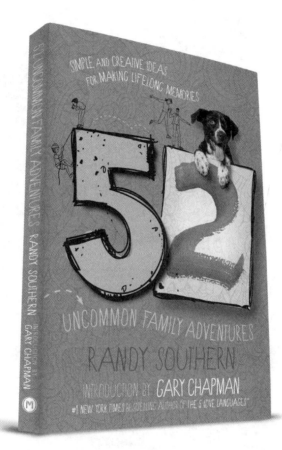

CREATE A LOVING AND SAFE ENVIRONMENT FOR YOUR BLENDED FAMILY